An introduction to

SOUTHWESTERN INDIAN ARTS & CRAFTS

D0725101

by TOM BAHTI

YAQUI PASCOLA MASK

Tom Bahti, a graduate of the Anthropology Department of the University of New Mexico, has been a dealer and collector of Indian art for the past fifteen years. Well-known in his field he has served numerous times as a judge at exhibits of Southwestern Indian arts and crafts, written articles and lectured on the subject.

Mr. Bahti's interest in Southwestern tribes is not limited to their crafts, however, as he is also active in several organizations which seek to improve the general welfare of the Indians through self-help programs.

An Arizonian by choice, he resides in Tucson where he owns and operates an Indian arts and crafts shop.

This booklet is dedicated to the Indian artisan who, in an age largely indifferent to his work, still finds the creation of handcrafts a rewarding experience. May his perseverance and integrity extend as far into the future as it does into the past.

Photography by K. CAMILLE DEN DOOVEN

SOUTHWESTERN INDIAN ARTS & CRAFTS, PUBLISHED BY KC PUBLICATIONS, BOX 428, FORT VALLEY ROAD, FLAGSTAFF, ARIZONA. ONE DOLLAR. L.C. NO. 65–449. COPYRIGHTED 1966 BY KC PUBLICATIONS.

Introduction

Beneath the gaudy and distracting surface of chicken feather warbonnets, beadwork from Hong Kong and quantities of imitation Indian jewelry can be found the strong and dignified craft traditions of the Southwest's original inhabitants.

It is not possible to fully appreciate these crafts without knowing something about them and the people who produce them. Nevertheless, even a casual observer can quickly learn to distinguish between cheap souvenirs and fine Indian work. Art cannot be entirely separated from culture, and the Southwest Indian has preserved more of his cultural traditions than he has lost.

The present-day crafts are living arts. Each has its own history of development. Some, such as basketry and pottery, can be traced back to hundreds of years before the Western Hemisphere was discovered. Others, such as silverwork and painting, are relatively recent and owe their existence to contact with the white foreigners.

Each craft has been subject to change brought about by the impact of new ideas, tools, materials or markets. Practicality is usually the main reason for change. It is practical, as an example, for a Navajo weaver to produce rugs for a non-Indian market and to purchase commercially made blankets for her own use when it means a new source of income. Simply because she uses little of her own work at home does not affect the authenticity of her product.

In each case, however, change was tailored to suit the native craftsman, and the ultimate result was unmistakably Indian.

Indian crafts have often been imitated both in this country and abroad. The Indian craftsman on the other hand has never felt the need or inclination to duplicate the work of others for the sake of a market.

This booklet is intended to serve the casual visitor to the Southwest as an introduction to the better-known crafts and to provide an understanding of the contributions of our Indians to the field of arts and crafts.

Notes & Comments

The following material is presented in an attempt to answer the questions most frequently asked by persons who are new to Indian art.

SYMBOLISM. Designs used to decorate pottery or baskets can often be identified as representations of clouds, rain, lightning, birds and the like. Similarly these designs may be used in silverwork and represent the same things. Beyond this, however, they have no "meanings" and are not symbols for ideas or words. The pattern used on a bracelet, for example, does not "tell a story." The mass of printed material which "interprets" Indian designs has no basis in fact. Some dealers in Indian art will invent a spurious story to go along with a craft item if they think it will encourage a buyer to make a purchase. Poor craftwork cannot be improved by the addition of a colorful story; fine craftwork will stand on its own merits.

ECONOMICS. The great majority of Indian craftsmen work at their trade on a purely part-time basis. Economically speaking, crafts are unimportant and account for probably less than one per cent of the total income received by Indians. Crafts are important, however, to the full-time craftsman and as an additional source of income to the part-time artist. Although economics plays an important role in the existence of a craft, it would be a mistake to consider the true value of arts and crafts in terms of only dollars and cents.

The most important ingredients in any craft, be it pottery or silver, are time and skill. We cannot judge the value of a product by the value of the materials used any more accurately than the price of a painting can be determined by the cost of the paint.

COMMERCIALISM. It is often said that commercialism is an evil that is ruining Indian art, and when a craftsman produces an item "just to sell" some intangible is lost that affects the genuineness of the product. The craftsman of any age produces items to sell or trade. When he is unable to barter his labor as a craftsman, he ceases to be one and must seek a livelihood at which he can earn a living. Neither does the Indian artist care whether his work is purchased by a tourist, collector or other Indian, for the identity of the purchaser does not affect the authenticity of his work.

BLACK POTTERY. Black pottery from the pueblos of Santa Clara and San Ildefonso is made of a native red clay that is polished before firing. The black finish is achieved during the firing by smothering the fire with powdered dung or shredded cedar bark. The black carbon smoke that results permeates the porous clay and turns it black.

CORAL. Gem coral or *coral rubrum,* a calcium carbonate colored by manganese, is formed by the skeletons of various marine organisms. It is found in the Mediterranean Sea in the vicinity of Sardinia and Corsica and off the west coast of Japan. The first coral used in the Southwest was brought in by the Spanish. It continues to be imported as a trade item to this day. There is no "prehistoric coral" in use. The pinkish-red beads found in archaeological sites, and mistakenly identified as coral, were made of stone.

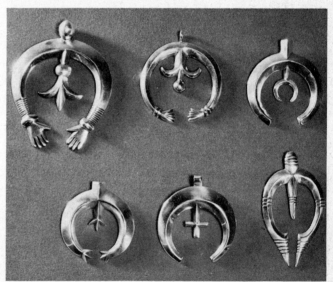

SANDCAST NAJAS

NAJA (na-zha). A Navajo word which refers to the crescent-shaped pendant used on both the squash blossom necklace and silver mounted bridle. This ornament was also used in the Middle East and North Africa as an amulet to ward off the evil eye. The Spanish copied this horse trapping from the Moors and brought it to the New World where it was adopted by the Indians. It appears today in the southwest in a great variety of forms but it is not regarded as a charm or amulet. The widely circulated stories which describe the naja and the squash blossom necklace as symbols of fertility are products of the whiteman's imagination and have no basis in Indian legends, beliefs or customs.

continued on page 7

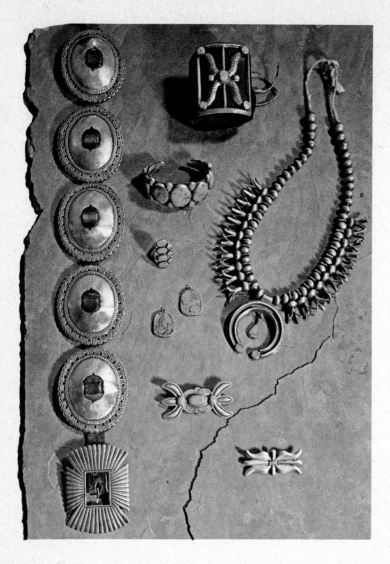

Silverwork

Because it is widely known, Indian silverwork is usually thought of as an ancient craft. Actually it is one of the most recent to be adopted by tribes in the Southwest.

The first silver ornaments used by the Southwestern Indians were obtained through trade or warfare with the Spanish or other tribes, depending upon which situation offered the greatest advantage at the moment.

In the mid-1800's it was the custom for Mexican smiths from the Rio Grande valley to roam through the Navajo country producing silver trinkets in exchange for horses. It was from these itinerant craftsmen that the Navajo first learned the art in the late 1850's.

The first pieces, made with crude homemade tools, were copies of the ornaments used by the early Spanish: domed buttons, hollow spherical beads, powder chargers, silver-mounted bridles and a small pomegranate, the forerunner of the well-known squash blossom. Bracelets, rings and conchos were copies of similar pieces used by the Plains Indians and obtained in trade from the Utes. Some early work was also done in copper and brass, but neither of these metals remained popular.

At first the craft was strictly an occupation of the men and passed from father to son or other close relatives. Occasionally an outsider might pay a smith to teach him the art, and in this way silversmithing spread from the Navajo to other tribes. The Zunis learned the craft in 1872, and by the 1890's most of the other pueblos had their own silversmiths.

Early silver jewelry was exclusively hammered work, usually light in weight because silver was scarce, decorated with simple incised or stamped designs. The craftsmen were quick to develop new techniques, to add new pieces to their repertoire and to adapt old items to new uses.

The squash blossom necklace provides the best example of an adapted item. Generally thought of as typically Indian, its individual parts can be traced to outside sources. The squash blossom is merely an elongated version of the small silver pomegranate once worn by the Spanish men as a trouser and cape ornament. The crescent-shaped pendant, or naja, originally appeared suspended from the center portion of the silver mounted bridle. This decoration came to the New World via Europe after the Spaniards borrowed it from the Moors of North Africa.

Tobacco canteens, bow guards, buckles and blouse ornaments were created in profusion as the use of silver by the Indians increased.

Coins provided the sole source of silver until 1890 when such use was prohibited by U. S. law. The Indian smiths continued using Mexican pesos until 1930 when Mexico forbade the export of its coin. Sterling silver in both slug and sheet form was then purchased by the white traders from silver refineries to sell to the craftsmen on the reservation. At no time did the Indians mine their own silver.

The first attempt to use turquoise settings was in 1880. Glass, jet and garnet were also tried but were not popular. Turquoise was used sparingly until the turn of the century when it became available in greater quantities. With the exception of Zuni work, most of the turquoise used today is cut and polished by non-Indians and furnished to the silversmiths, in cabachon form, ready for mounting. *continued on page 6*

NAVAJO — typical Navajo work is noted for its massive quality and simplicity of design. Turquoise sets are used primarily to enhance the beauty of the silver. Recently new techniques have been added; overlay, usually thought of as Hopi, and channel, generally associated with the Zuni, are now being produced by the Navajo. Sandcasting, begun in 1875, continues to be popular along with hammered, filed and stamped work.

ZUNI — the cutting and setting of stones for which the Zuni are so well known was not begun until 1890, eighteen years after they learned to work in silver. Until that time their work closely resembled the Navajo styles. Multiple rows of turquoise in bracelets and clustered sets in pins and rings soon became popular. Multicolored inlay of jet, shell and turquoise was started in 1935 and channel work in the early 1940's. The outstanding trait of Zuni work is that it emphasizes the use of stones rather than the silver.

HOPI — from the late 1890's until 1938 the Hopi silversmiths followed the traditions of Navajo and Zuni work . In 1938 a program instituted by the Museum of Northern Arizona encouraged Hopi smiths to develop a style of silverwork based on their distinctive pottery designs and executed in an overlay technique. The experiment was so successful that most Hopi silver workers continue to follow this new trend. Sandcast silver is also produced by a few silversmiths.

5

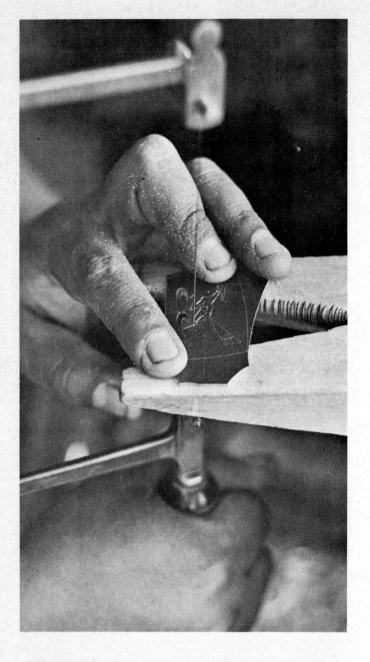

SILVERWORK, continued.

Until the late 1890's all of the work produced was for the Indian market. Then the railroad brought the white man and a second market was catered to. Orders from curio companies created a demand for lightweight pins, bracelets and rings decorated with crossed arrows, swastikas and thunderbirds. Salad sets, spoons, cuff links, tie bars and other hitherto unknown pieces were made to meet the demands of the new market.

Both markets, Indian and non-Indian, continue today; both change due to changes in styles, fashions, fads and usage. Neither can be said to be superior in design or quality. A Navajo silversmith may produce a fine heavy sandcast bracelet for a white customer and prefer to wear a Zuni bracelet with elaborate clusters of turquoise himself. Nothing is as constant as change and custom needs no reason.

Silversmithing is one of the very few native trades at which a craftsman, employed full-time, can earn a living. Nevertheless, most of the work produced is the result of part-time labor and usually provides a relatively small part of the craftsman's total income.

Many people lament the passing of "fine old silverwork" but the truth of the matter is that more fine work is being produced today than at any single time in the past. This is partly the result of new and better tools but also because the craftsman himself is constantly striving to improve his work in both design and technique.

SUGGESTED READING

ADAIR, JOHN. *The Navajo and Pueblo Silversmiths*, University of Oklahoma Press, Norman, Oklahoma. 1944.

COLTON, MARY RUSSELL F. "Hopi Silversmithing, Its Background and Future," *Plateau*, Vol. XII, No. 1, Museum of Northern Arizona. July, 1939.

MERA, HARRY P. *Indian Silverwork of the Southwest, Illustrated*, Dale Stuart King, Publisher. Globe, Arizona. 1960.

NEUMANN, DAVID L. "Navaho Channel Turquoise and Silver," *El Palacio*, Vol. 61, No. 12. Santa Fe. 1954.

WOODWARD, ARTHUR. "A Brief History of Navajo Silversmithing," *Bulletin No. 14*. Museum of Northern Arizona. Flagstaff, Arizona. 1946.

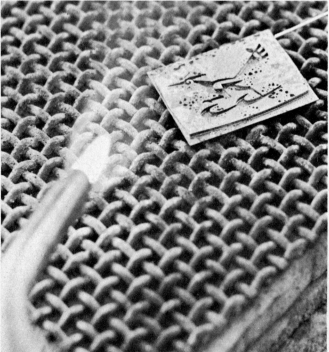

TOP. *A Hopi silversmith uses a jeweler's saw to cut out the design for an overlay belt buckle.*
BOTTOM. *A torch is used to "sweat" the cut out portion onto a solid sheet of silver.*

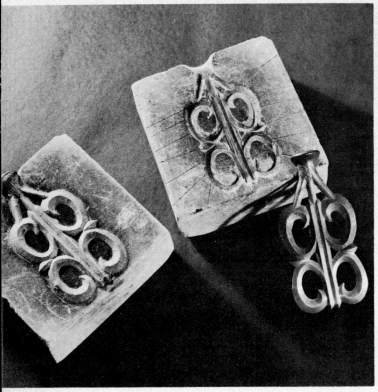

TUFA MOLD AND CASTINGS   SANDCAST JEWELRY

NOTES & COMMENTS, continued.

SANDCASTING. Sandcasting makes use of a mold of soft volcanic pumice or tufa. A piece of tufa is ground to a smooth surface and the design carved into it with a knife or a file. Care must be taken to design it properly so that the silver will flow into all the carved areas of the mold. Air vents are scratched into the surface to prevent the formation of air pockets which would ruin the casting. The mold is then smoked to allow the silver to flow freely over the carbonized surface. A flat slab of pumice, also smoked, is then placed on top of the carved section and wired in place. Silver is melted in a pottery crucible and poured into the mold.

The resulting casting, triangular in cross-section, is very rough and must be filed and polished. Bracelets are cast flat and later shaped by hammering.

Sandcasting is one of the most difficult of silverworking techniques. Relatively few silversmiths are skilled in this work.

Commercial casting compounds are sometimes used today instead of tufa in the production of small pins.

CHANNEL WORK. A term applied to the setting of turquoise or other stone or shell into a silver base. The silver frame which holds the stones is constructed in the manner of an egg carton. Each stone is cut to fit into its separate compartment. The stones are then cemented into place and the entire piece is ground and polished to present a smooth and even surface. A nugget finish can also be achieved using the same basic technique.

INLAY. A Zuni stoneworking technique in which a mosaic of stones is enclosed in a bezel of silver and mounted on a silver plate. This work is related to a prehistoric technique of setting turquoise, shell or jet on a base of wood, bone or shell. This style of ornamentation is still used for pendants and earrings. In early days piñon pitch was used to hold the stones in place. Today commercial adhesives are used.

OVERLAY. Overlay is a silverworking technique in which two sheets of silver are used. The design is cut out of one with a jeweler's saw and overlaid on the solid piece. The two pieces are then "sweated" together. The bottom portion is then turned black with liver of sulfur to make the design stand out. After shaping and polishing, the finished piece gives the appearance of having been carved from a single sheet of heavy silver.

continued on page 30

Pawn

To the Indian a trading post is more than just a place to buy and sell goods. It is a social center, a post office and an employment agency; in addition to this it also serves as a hock shop and the local bank. The trader performs all of the services of these two latter institutions through a transaction known as pawning.

A wad of bills, though admittedly practical, is not particularly attractive from an aesthetic point of view, so most Indians convert their

pawn the items for a dollar or two and pay the interest rate in return for this safety deposit box service.

If an item is not redeemed after the agreed-upon length of time, it becomes "dead pawn" and may be sold by the trader for whatever amount it will bring.

Saddles, Pendleton shawls, saddle blankets, buckskins, rifles and baskets are also pawned in addition to jewelry.

NAVAJO WOMAN REDEEMS HER NECKLACE FROM TRADING POST VAULT

ready cash into silver and turquoise jewelry. When in need of money or credit, they will take a bracelet or a belt to the trader and use it as security for a loan.

At a specified date the loan is repaid in full plus interest, and the jewelry is redeemed or a new arrangement is made to renew the loan.

Oftentimes a Navajo has no need for a loan but merely wants a safe place in which to keep his most valuable jewelry. In this case he may

SUGGESTED READING

ADAMS, WILLIAM Y. "Shonto: A Study of the Role of the Trader in a Modern Navajo Community," *Smithsonian Institution. B. A. E. Bulletin 188.* 1963.

GILLMOR, FRANCES, AND WETHERILL, LOUISA WADE. *Traders to the Navajos,* U. of New Mexico Press, Albuquerque, New Mexico. 1952.

HEGEMANN, ELIZABETH C. *Navaho Trading Days,* University of New Mexico Press, Albuquerque, New Mexico. 1963.

MC NITT, FRANK. *The Indian Traders,* University of Oklahoma Press, Norman, Oklahoma. 1962.

MOUNTAIN LION   MOUNTAIN LION   EAGLE   BUFFALO   HORSE   RAM   SHEEP
EAGLE   SHEEP
BEAR   BEAR   MOLE   PRAYER STICK
BEAR   WOLF   WOLF
WOLF

Zuni Fetishes

The use of fetishes by southwestern Indians is of prehistoric origin. Any object may be used as a fetish; arrow points, concretions, shells or plants. A spirit is believed to dwell in the object which can give assistance, in the form of supernatural power, to its owner.

Fetishes may be the property of households, clans, kivas or individuals. They are treated with reverence and when not in actual use are carefully stored in fetish jars and ceremonially "fed" with cornmeal or pollen. Large fetishes may serve as altar pieces. Others are used in curing rites, war ceremonies, witchcraft or farming. Some are carried as gambling charms or aids in hunting. The Zunis make most of the fetishes used in the Southwest today and are highly respected by other tribes for their ability to carve them.

The most common fetishes seen on the market are the ones used for hunting. They may be carved from shell, stone or antler. The pieces most highly prized by the Indians are natural stone formations which bear a resemblance to a specific animal. The use of these carvings by the Zuni is traced back to a legend which tells of a time when all animals were turned into stone by certain gods. All hunting fetishes are regarded as representations of these original petrified animals. The power derived from these beasts assists the hunter in pursuit of game.

Each cardinal direction (the Zuni recognize six) has its corresponding animal; the hunter of the North is the mountain lion, easily identified by its long tail curled flat over its back; West is represented by either the bear or coyote; South is the wild cat; East is the wolf; the Zenith is the eagle; and the Nadir is the mole.

Beads of shell, coral or turquoise, feathers or a small carving in the form of an arrow point may be tied to these stone animals to increase their power or as offerings to the fetish in return for favors granted.

SUGGESTED READING

CUSHING, FRANK H. "Zuni Fetishes," *2nd Annual Report, B. A. E.*, pp. 9-45, Washington. 1883.

KIRK, RUTH F. *Introduction to Zuni Fetishism*, Papers of the School of American Research. Santa Fe. 1943.

BEAR FETISH

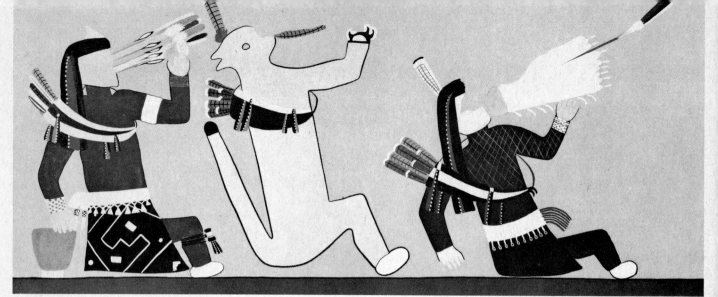

Reproduction of a prehistoric kiva wall mural from Pottery Mound, New Mexico, depicts a mountain lion and hunters. This painting, executed in earth pigments on a plaster wall, is one of a series excavated by the Anthropology Department of the University of New Mexico.

Earth painting by Pablita Velarde of Santa Clara pueblo uses the same basic techniques as the kiva mural shown above. The design is adapted from early paintings excavated at Kuaua near Bernalillo, New Mexico.

Painting

Painting on paper is the most recent art expression to be adopted by the Southwestern Indians. Painting itself, however, was an old technique long before the Spaniards arrived. Hide, wood, pottery, stone, textiles and the plastered walls of ceremonial chambers were decorated with paints made from earth and vegetable pigments.

The use of commercial watercolors and paper began shortly after the turn of the century. The first artists, from the pueblo of San Ildefonso, were encouraged by teachers and anthropoligists to take up this new medium. The earliest subjects depicted were usually ceremonial dancers.

Among the earliest artists were Awa Tsireh, Crescencio Martinez and Tonita Pena of San Ildefonso Pueblo, Fred Kabotie and Otis Polelonema from the Hopi villages and Ma-pe-wi of Zia.

In 1932 the Bureau of Indian Affairs established at the Santa Fe Indian School an experimental class designed to instruct young Indian students in the use of the new medium. This program was successful and Indian painting was soon accepted as a new artistic expression both in this country and abroad.

With the exception of Hopi painting, which employs modeling and shading, all of the work tends to be highly decorative, two-dimensional and executed in a flat, opaque watercolor technique. All painting is done from memory and models are not used. Rain, sun, clouds and lightning are usually depicted by symbols even when the main subject of the painting is treated realistically.

Recent work by young artists shows a dissatisfaction with the restrictions imposed by the "traditional" flat watercolor medium and a desire to experiment with new techniques.

SUGGESTED READING

DUNN, DOROTHY. "America's First Painters," *The National Geographic Magazine.* March, 1955.

DUTTON, BERTHA. *Sun Father's Way,* University of New Mexico Press, Albuquerque. 1963.

SMITH, WATSON. "Kiva Mural Decorations at Awatovi and Kawaika-a," *Papers of the Peabody Museum,* Harvard University, Vol. XXXVII, Cambridge. 1952.

TANNER, CLARA LEE. *Southwest Indian Painting,* University of Arizona Press, Tucson. 1957.

ANDY TSINAJINNIE

HARRISON BEGAY

R. C. GORMAN

CHARLIE LEE

BEATIN YAZZ

RAY NAHA

11

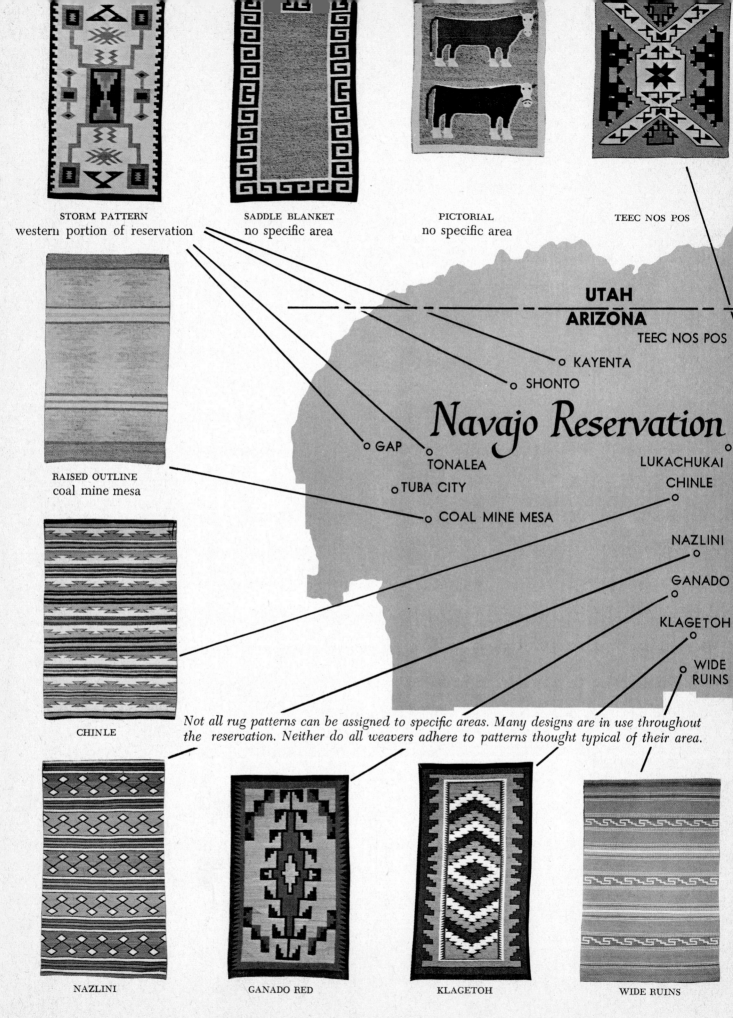

STORM PATTERN
western portion of reservation

SADDLE BLANKET
no specific area

PICTORIAL
no specific area

TEEC NOS POS

UTAH
ARIZONA

TEEC NOS POS

○ KAYENTA

○ SHONTO

Navajo Reservation

○ GAP

○ TONALEA

○ LUKACHUKAI

CHINLE
○

○ TUBA CITY

○ COAL MINE MESA

NAZLINI
○

GANADO
○

KLAGETOH
○

WIDE
RUINS
○

RAISED OUTLINE
coal mine mesa

CHINLE

Not all rug patterns can be assigned to specific areas. Many designs are in use throughout the reservation. Neither do all weavers adhere to patterns thought typical of their area.

NAZLINI

GANADO RED

KLAGETOH

WIDE RUINS

TWILLED WEAVE
no specific area

TWO GRAY HILLS

ORADO
W MEXICO

SHIPROCK

TWO GRAY
HILLS

YEI or CEREMONIAL
lukachukai and shiprock

CRYSTAL

CRYSTAL

GALLUP

THROW
gallup area

TWO FACED
no specific area

Navajo Weaving

The Navajo, numbering about 80,000 people, is the largest tribe in the United States. Relative newcomers to the Southwest, they changed from hunters and gatherers to semi-nomadic herders following the acquisition of livestock from the Spanish.

With sheep obtained from the Spanish and the technique of weaving learned from the pueblo Indians, the Navajo soon became widely known for their blankets and rugs.

From 1700 A. D. until the introduction of machine-made fabric in the late 1800's, the Navajo were best known for their finely woven blankets. This craft began to decline as commercial clothing became available. Rather than let weaving die out completely, the white traders urged the Navajo women to make heavier pieces that would be suitable for floor coverings.

With this change in weight and use came changes in pattern and color. Large geometric designs with borders and a wide variety of commercial dyes replaced the earlier simple striped patterns in limited colors. The traders correctly assumed these would appeal to the new non-Indian market.

After much experimenting, rugs of good quality were produced. Regional differences in design and color became apparent as weavers specialized in producing patterns requested by the traders in their areas.

Rug designs are without significance although some patterns have acquired names through common usage. The so-called ceremonial rug, for example, uses design elements adapted from sandpaintings, but the rug itself is not used in any part of a Navajo rite and is not "ceremonial" in any sense of the word.

There is a decided trend toward vegetable dye rugs. This began in the 1930's when several

of the loud commercial dyes. The revival was highly successful and numerous vegetable dyes previously unknown were developed through experimentation by the weavers. About eighty dye recipes, utilizing a wide variety of plants, berries, bark, fruit, roots and flowers, are used today.

The casual visitor seldom realizes the hours of labor involved in making a rug. The wool must first be clipped from the sheep, then washed, carded, spun into yarn and dyed. The amount of labor expended in preparing the yarn for a rug is often greater than the time spent in the actual weaving process. After this the loom is prepared and the weaver, without any pattern or visual aid, begins to weave.

A three-foot by five-foot rug of average quality requires about 350 hours' work. The time naturally increases with the fineness of the yarn and the weave. The preparation of native dyes also adds hours to a rug.

Needless to say, no Navajo weaver can earn a living at her craft. Neither can a non-Indian earn a livelihood by knitting socks. Both crafts continue as avocations rather than occupations.

Navajo rugs are justly famous not only for their beauty but their durability. It is the hand-spun yarn that gives these rugs their strength. It is not uncommon for a rug to last 30 to 40 years. This should be an important consideration in determining the true value of a Navajo rug.

Weaving continues to decline with each passing year as far as quantity is concerned. Quality remains high. *continued on page 31*

SPINNING YARN

In most pueblo homes a long pole is suspended from the roof beams and used as a hanger for a wide variety of native garments.

The weaving of cotton in the Southwest predates the arrival of the Spaniards by 900 years. Among the pueblo people weaving is the traditional occupation of the men. This craft has disappeared completely in a number of the pueblo tribes, and they now rely upon the Hopis to supply them, through trade, with ceremonial

garments. Most of these items are made of cotton and decorated with wool yarn. The items shown here are (L to R): brocaded sash and embroidered kilt worn by male dancers, boy's woolen plaid blanket woven in a diamond twill, a braided "rain" or wedding sash of cotton and a woman's belt of commercially dyed wool. The embroidered kilt (second from left) is shown in greater detail on page 2.

How to buy Indian crafts

Every art has its imitators and Indian art is no exception. Because of its broad market, Indian jewelry is the craft most often imitated. Misleading advertising is responsible for much of the sale of the spurious article. It is well to remember that the words "Indian design" or "Indian style" used in a display of jewelry is no promise that the items shown are actually handmade by Indian craftsman. Similarly, "silver metal" and "turquoise blue stone" are descriptive phrases and do not necessarily mean that the materials described are either sterling silver or genuine turquoise.

A purchase made directly from an Indian is not always a guarantee of authenticity. Many a dimestore imitation has been bought by the uninitiated from perfectly genuine Indians who roam the streets in search of an unwary visitor. Persons who would never think of buying a diamond from a street corner vendor will not hesitate to purchase plastic and pot metal jewelry if the seller is picturesque enough.

Obviously no one can become an expert on Indian crafts during a short trip to the southwest. It is therefore necessary to rely on dealers who have a reputation for handling authentic Indian crafts. The local Chamber of Commerce or museum are often good places to inquire after the names of reputable shops.

Care of Indian crafts

NAVAJO RUGS should be cleaned by vacuuming or sweeping and not shaken with a whip-like action. This "snapping" motion tends to fray the edges and break the warp threads.

It is advisable to place a pad under a rug used on a bare floor to prevent it from sliding. A pad will also increase the life of the rug. Reverse a rug occasionally to permit both sides to wear uniformly.

Spots can be removed with a naptha solvent. Overall cleaning can be done with a good rug shampoo but keep in mind that wool shrinks and stretches and the rug must be laid out flat to dry.

continued on page 31

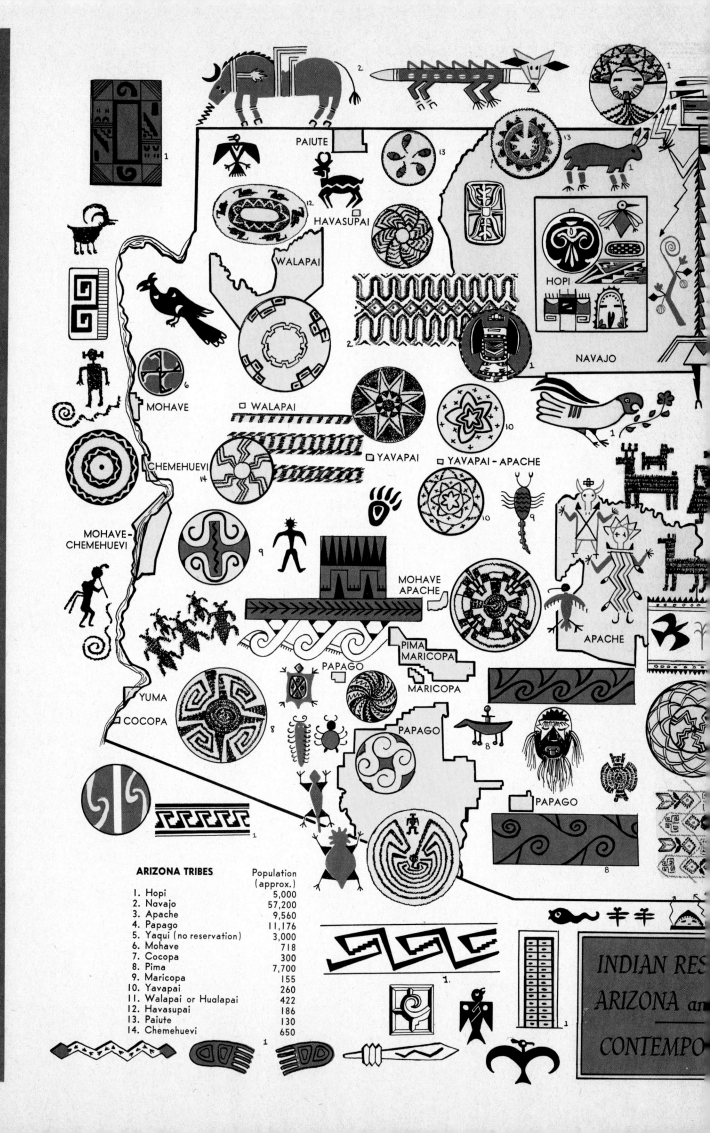

PAIUTE

HAVASUPAI

WALAPAI

MOHAVE

CHEMEHUEVI

MOHAVE-
CHEMEHUEVI

☐ WALAPAI

☐ YAVAPAI

☐ YAVAPAI - APACHE

MOHAVE
APACHE

PIMA
MARICOPA

MARICOPA

PAPAGO

YUMA

COCOPA

HOPI

NAVAJO

APACHE

PAPAGO

ARIZONA TRIBES

		Population (approx.)
1.	Hopi	5,000
2.	Navajo	57,200
3.	Apache	9,560
4.	Papago	11,176
5.	Yaqui (no reservation)	3,000
6.	Mohave	718
7.	Cocopa	300
8.	Pima	7,700
9.	Maricopa	155
10.	Yavapai	260
11.	Walapai or Hualapai	422
12.	Havasupai	186
13.	Paiute	130
14.	Chemehuevi	650

INDIAN RES

ARIZONA an

CONTEMPO

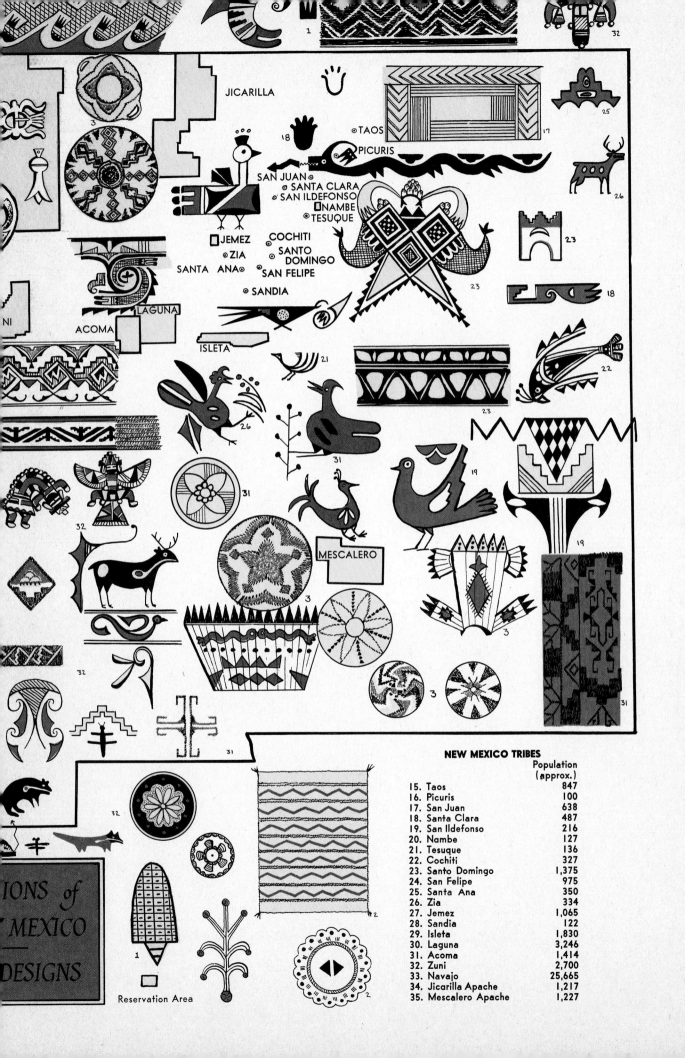

JICARILLA

TAOS

PICURIS

SAN JUAN
SANTA CLARA
SAN ILDEFONSO
NAMBE
TESUQUE

JEMEZ   COCHITI
    ZIA   SANTO
SANTA ANA   DOMINGO
         SAN FELIPE

         SANDIA

NI

LAGUNA

ACOMA

ISLETA

MESCALERO

NEW MEXICO TRIBES

		Population (approx.)
15.	Taos	847
16.	Picuris	100
17.	San Juan	638
18.	Santa Clara	487
19.	San Ildefonso	216
20.	Nambe	127
21.	Tesuque	136
22.	Cochiti	327
23.	Santo Domingo	1,375
24.	San Felipe	975
25.	Santa Ana	350
26.	Zia	334
27.	Jemez	1,065
28.	Sandia	122
29.	Isleta	1,830
30.	Laguna	3,246
31.	Acoma	1,414
32.	Zuni	2,700
33.	Navajo	25,665
34.	Jicarilla Apache	1,217
35.	Mescalero Apache	1,227

IONS of

MEXICO

DESIGNS

Reservation Area

TWO GRAY HILLS RUG
DAISY TAUGELCHEE
Navajo

HUTUTU, SAYATASHA, WOLF KACHINAS
OTTO PENTEWA *Hopi*

The individual in Indian art

When dealing with native arts there is always a tendency to think of the craftsmen as an anonymous group rather than as individuals. Within an Indian craft tradition highly individualistic expressions are possible.

HORSEHAIR BASKET
ROSE MIKE *Papago*

FIGURINE — SARAH GARCIA
BOWL — LUCY LEWIS *Acoma*

POTTERY DOLLS
ANNIE FIELDS *Mojave*

WHEELMADE VASE & SANDCAST JEWELRY
CHARLES LOLOMA *Hopi*

BLACK WARE
MARIA MARTINEZ
San Ildefonso

WOODCARVING
TOM YAZZIE *Navajo*

SANDPAINTING
FRED STEVENS
Navajo

SPLIT STITCH BASKETS
MARY MIGUEL *Papago*

POTTERY
FANNIE & ELVA NAMPEYO *Hopi*

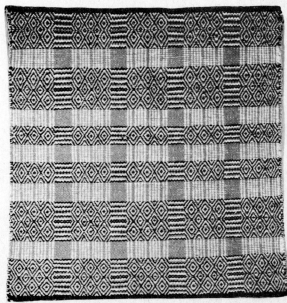

TWILLED WEAVE SADDLE BLANKET
DOROTHY WILSON *Navajo*

HEMIS

TAWA
sun

KOKOPELI MANA

TALAVI
early morning

KOYEMSI
mudhead

The Hopi word *kachina* is used in three ways. It may refer to (1) the supernatural beings, (2) the male dancers who impersonate these deities or (3) the painted wooden dolls which are representations of the masked dancers.

The importance of the kachina in the religious life of the ancient pueblo people is indicated by the numerous depictions of their masks on pottery vessels, in kiva murals and on canyon walls throughout the Southwest. Today kachinas appear in the ceremonies of most pueblos but are more prevalent among the Hopi and Zuni villages.

The kachina is an old concept, but the kachina doll is not. It is probably less than one hundred years old. These dolls are not idols and are not worshipped or prayed to. They are used in the religious training of the young children to teach them the characteristics and names of over two hundred individual kachinas which they will see during their lifetime. The children receive the dolls as gifts from the masked dancers who appear in the villages during the kachina ceremonies.

Many persons are astonished to learn that the Hopi have 250 kachinas and cannot imagine why there is a need for so many. Similarly, the

AVACHOYA
spotted corn

KWA—eagle

KWEO—wolf

HAKTO

CHAVEYO
black ogre

MONGWA
owl

AYA
rattle

HAHAI WUUQTI
kachina mother

Hopi fail to understand why Christians should have a need for their 30,000 saints. The comparison is appropriate, for the functions of the saint and the kachina are roughly parallel in their respective religions. Each serves as a go-between for mortals and the more important deities. Persons unfamiliar with Southwestern art often find the kachina doll grotesque in appearance. It is well to remember, however, that an Indian's first view of a crucifix may evoke the same reaction.

The Hopi men carve kachina dolls from the root of the cottonwood tree. They use a knife and rasp to form the figure and a small piece of sandstone to smooth it. The figure is then covered with a light coating of kaolin, a white clay, and painted in the likeness of the kachina it is intended to portray. Earth pigments used to decorate early dolls have given way to commercial poster paints which offer a much wider range of color.

The dolls vary from simple flat slab form, the kind given to

clowns climbing pole

steps in carving a kachina doll

HOPI KACHINA DOLL MAKER

lenge the men of the village to foot races and reward them with gifts if they win. Young boys are encouraged to become good runners, for if the kachina wins a race, he may cut the loser's hair or rub his face with soot.

Many of the female kachinas, a role played by the men also, provide musical accompaniment with gourds and rasping sticks for the dancers.

The kachinas are believed to live on the San Francisco Peaks north of Flagstaff, Arizona. At the time of the winter solstice they leave their homes to visit the Hopi villages where they dance for the people. One of the purposes of these ceremonies is to bring rain to help the crops grow but their main purpose is to promote the general well-being of the people. The benefit is not limited to the Hopi, however, for they believe that a kachina dance performed in the proper spirit extends its blessings far beyond the borders of their reservation.

The kachina season ends with the Niman or Home Dance in late July and marks the return of the kachinas to the San Francisco mountains until the following year.

infants, to elaborately carved figures in dance poses. Simple figures are often carved from a single piece of wood. The more intricate dolls are generally made of smaller pieces fitted together with tiny wooden pegs.

Kachinas are the spirits of birds, animals, insects, plants, places, objects or people. Each has a name, often that of the item it represents: owl, roadrunner, wolf, horse, cricket, chili, Sunset Crater, rattle, snow or thunder. Often the name cannot be translated or is merely the distinctive call of the particular kachina.

Many of the kachinas have well-defined functions and may be warriors or hunters. Some have the power to cure specific maladies such as epilepsy or rheumatism. One group, the clowns,

SUGGESTED READING

COLTON, HAROLD S. *Hopi Kachina Dolls*, University of New Mexico Press, Revised ed., Albuquerque. 1959.

DOCKSTADER, FREDERICK J. "The Kachina and the White Man," *Cranbrook Institute of Science, Bulletin 35.* 1954.

WRIGHT, BARTON AND ROAT, EVELYN. *This Is a Hopi Kachina*, Museum of Northern Arizona, Flagstaff. 1962.

Navajo women adapted their present costume from a Civil War era fashion worn by the wives of officers stationed at military posts in the southwest. Generally thought of as being "typically Indian" the Navajo dress was recently re-adapted by white designers as the popular "squaw dress". PHOTOGRAPH BY DON ARMOUR

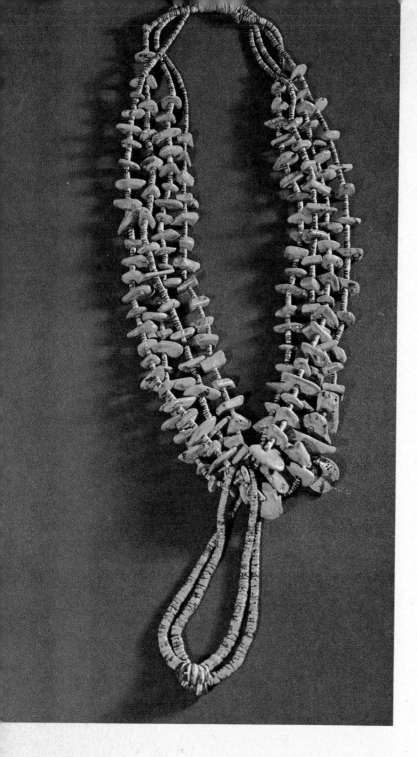

Turquoise

Turquoise, a hydrous aluminum phosphate colored by copper salts, is a semi-precious stone generally found in the arid regions of the world. It is highly prized in India, Persia and China in addition to the American Southwest, where it has been used since 500 A. D. Its primary use is for personal adornment, but it also serves as offerings to important deities and is sometimes crushed for use in sandpaintings.

Turquoise is deposited by water action and is found in veins in other rock. This matrix, or mother rock, is responsible for the markings in turquoise. The matrix may be thin black lines, brown or black blotches, iron pyrites or bits of quartz. The color of turquoise may run from a pale chalky blue to a dark green with literally dozens of shades in between. The quality and price of a stone depend upon its color, hardness and matrix. Its value will range from a few cents a carat in the poorer grades to over two dollars a carat in the finest. The most highly prized stone is a deep blue color with a dark spider-web matrix. It should be remembered, however, that both color and markings are purely a matter of personal preference.

Hard stones are preferred because they are less likely to change color. Prolonged or repeated contact with soap or body oils will change the color of softer stones to a dark green.

In pre-Spanish times the Indians mined turquoise with hammers of stone and picks made of antler. Fire was also used to crack the rock containing the blue gem. The largest of the early mines is located near Cerrillos, New Mexico. It extends two hundred feet underground and is three hundred feet wide in places.

Today turquoise is mined on a small scale in Colorado, New Mexico, Arizona and Nevada. None of these mines are owned by Indians.

SUGGESTED READING

NEUMANN, DAVID. "Turquoise," *El Palacio*, Vol. 59, No. 10. October, 1952.

POGUE, JOSEPH E. "The Turquoise," *Memoirs of the National Academy of Sciences*, XII, Part II, Third Memoir. Washington. 1915.

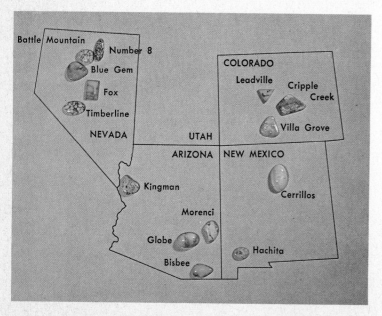

Turquoise samples mark the locations of the better known mines in the southwest.

Papago baskets (L to R) 1 and 2 — coiled work of bleached yucca and devil's claw, 3 and 4 — coiled bird figurines, 5 — split stitch tray, 6 — plaited covered basket of palm leaves, 7 — double coil tray, 8 — devil's claw bowl, 9 and 10 — willow and devil's claw bowls.

Hopi baskets (L to R) 1 thru 4 — wicker work from Third Mesa, 5 — plaited sifter basket made on all Mesas, 6 thru 10 — coiled work from Second Mesa.

Baskets

Considered from a purely economic standpoint, basketry should have disappeared completely many years ago. Fifteen cents an hour is hardly an incentive to pursue this craft, and few weavers ever earn more than this. Being the oldest of all present-day crafts, however, it is not surprising to find that the importance of baskets in the everyday and ceremonial life of the Indians far exceeds their monetary value.

Most Navajo curing rites require the use of a basket in some portion of the ceremony. The Hopi present coiled plaques to the winners of foot races. Sifter baskets are in daily use in Hopi homes. Payment for work performed is often made with baskets. Even among tribes in which the art has disappeared, baskets are in great demand, and a lively trade exists between them and weavers of other areas.

Few people appreciate baskets as the Indians do, for few people realize the time and skill that go into making them. A basketmaker must know the seasons for gathering her materials, how to harvest, dry, preserve and prepare them for use in addition to knowing the intricate techniques for the actual construction of a basket.

continued on next page

YAVAPAI

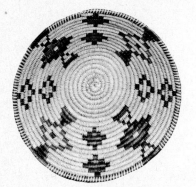

JICARILLA APACHE

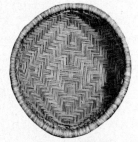

JEMEZ

SANTA DOMINGO — COCHITI

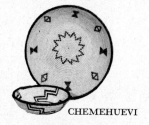

CHEMEHUEVI

HAVASUPAI

Gathering materials alone can be a time-consuming process. It is not uncommon for a Papago weaver to travel over two hundred miles to obtain her materials.

With the exception of plaited yucca baskets from Jemez and a limited number of coiled baskets made by the Jicarilla Apaches, most of the work in New Mexico is limited to open wicker-work bowls of willow produced at a few of the central Rio Grande pueblos.

The Indians of Arizona produce a much greater quantity and variety of work. The Hopis of Third Mesa make wicker trays, bowls and wastebaskets of rabbit brush or sumac colored with either aniline or native dyes. Second Mesa villages produce tightly woven coiled plaques and baskets of grass sewn with narrow strips of native-dyed yucca. The villages of all three of the Hopi mesas use plaited yucca sifter baskets constructed over a willow ring. This style of basket dates back about 1500 years. The Hopis themselves are the greatest users of their own baskets, but they also produce a surplus to sell or trade.

PAPAGO BASKET WEAVER

The Papagos of Southern Arizona make more baskets than any other tribe in the United States. During 1963 an estimated 8,000 baskets were produced by weavers ranging in age from 5 years to 87 years.

A typical Papago basket is constructed of a coil of bear grass sewn with bleached yucca and the black outer covering of the devil's claw seed pod. Green and yellow, also yucca, and red, obtained from the roots of the narrow leaf yucca, Spanish Dagger or desert willow are also used to add a variety of color. No dyes are used. Designs are usually simple geometric patterns or figures of animals or humans. Figurines of animals, birds, and humans are also made in coiled work.

Recently there has been a revival of the old style baskets made of cattails sewn with willow and devil's claw. Miniatures made of yucca, willow or horsehair have also staged a comeback.

Basket prices are determined by the fineness of the weave, the number of stitches per inch, the evenness of the shape and the complexity of the design. As with most things, the more time and skill that go into them, the more they will cost.

The Western Apaches, famous for their finely-designed bowl baskets, produce little today beyond an occasional piñon-pitch covered *tus* or water bottle and burden basket decorated with long buckskin fringes.

The Havasupais, Hualapais, Yavapais, Paiutes, Pimas and Chemehuevis all produce baskets but in very limited quantities.

SUGGESTED READING

COLTON, MARY RUSSELL. "The Arts and Crafts of the Hopi Indians," Museum of Northern Arizona. *Museum Notes Vol. II,* 1-24, Flagstaff, Arizona. 1938.

EVANS, GLEN T. AND T. N. CAMPBELL. *Indian Baskets,* Texas Memorial Museum. Austin. 1952.

MASON, OTIS T. "Aboriginal American Basketry," U. S. National Museum. *Annual Report,* 1902.

ROBINSON, BERT. *The Basket Weavers of Arizona,* University of New Mexico Press. Albuquerque, 1954.

UNDERHILL, RUTH. *Pueblo Crafts,* U. S. Dept. of the Interior, Haskell Institute. Lawrence, Kansas. 1944.

PIMA

MESCALERO APACHE

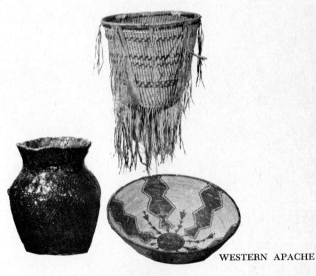

WESTERN APACHE

NAVAJO — PAIUTE

PAPAGO MINIATURES

MOJAVE — *there is only one surviving potter in this tribe. She produces human figurines, frogs, small effigy jars, pipes and ladles decorated in traditional designs.*

SANTA CLARA — *polished red ware, often decorated with designs in bluish-gray and white, and black ware finished in a high polish or painted with designs in matte black are the most commonly produced. Animal and bird figurines are prevalent.*

SAN ILDEFONSO — *highly polished red and black ware with matte designs became popular in 1920. Carved ware was begun in the early 1930's. Pottery from Santa Clara and San Ildefonso pueblos are identical in appearance.*

TAOS AND PICURIS — *a micaceous clay used in the slip gives this pottery a golden glitter. This ware is well-fired and much sought after for use as cooking vessels. A wide-mouthed bean pot is the most popular form of culinary ware.*

PAPAGO — *rough-textured water ollas, some of considerable capacity, and polished ware decorated with simple geometric patterns in black are traditional with the Papagos. A limited amount of black-on-white pottery is also made.*

LAGUNA — *is very similar to Acoma pottery in both form and design but is much heavier walled and usually not as carefully decorated. Almost no pottery is produced today at this pueblo.*

COCHITI — *jars, bowls and vessels in the form of birds are decorated with designs representing lightning, clouds and rain. Humorous figurines of people, frogs and animals are produced in a great variety.*

HOPI — *in addition to decorative pieces made for sale or trade, the Hopi use a considerable amount of their pottery for cooking ware. With the exception of an undecorated utility ware from the village of Hotevilla, all Hopi pottery is produced on First Mesa.*

PIMA — *a polished red ware decorated with simple designs is produced in a limited quantity. In shape, form, and finish, this pottery is very similar to Papago work.*

SANTO DOMINGO — *very little of the traditional pottery shown here is made today. Most of the present work is merely copied from popular styles of other pueblos. A poor grade of polished red and black ware is decorated with white house paint.*

ZUNI — *owl figurines are the best-known pieces from this pueblo. A few bowls and jars are still made but most of the women have turned from pottery to the more lucrative craft of silversmithing.*

NAVAJO — *these crude cooking pots receive a coating of piñon pitch after firing. The round or pointed bottom shape is easier to place in a campfire than a wide, flat-bottomed container. Small crucibles for melting silver and ceremonial pipes are also made occasionally.*

MARICOPA — *finely made bowls and long-necked jars with a highly polished red finish are typical of the work of Maricopa potters.*

SAN JUAN — *the most common types are a plain polished red, a light brown incised ware made of a clay which contains mica, and a rough-textured polychrome. Decorative plates carved in low relief are also popular.*

ZIA — *stylized floral patterns, realistically painted deer and conventionalized birds are the favorite designs used at this pueblo. Large storage jars are still made on occasion.*

ACOMA — *is the thinnest-walled and lightest in weight of all modern pottery. There is a recent trend toward reproducing prehistoric ceramic forms and designs. Figurines of birds and animals are also popular.*

Pottery

The art of pottery making in the Southwest is about 1600 years old. Early pieces were used as storage jars, cooking pots and ceremonial vessels. Both form and design varied from one tribe to the next just as they do today. Change was the rule rather than the exception. Archaeologists use a chronology based on the variations in pottery types as a method of dating prehistoric ruins.

The introduction of metal containers had a great effect on the ceramic arts. Large storage jars were seldom produced, and the use of cooking vessels was sharply reduced. At the same time the demand, by non-Indians, for small decorative pieces increased and pottery production was tailored to fit this new market.

Modern pottery sold to the tourist is made in the same manner as the prehistoric ware. It is authentic Indian work in every sense. Clay is dug from local deposits, ground and refined and mixed with a grit or temper. Pottery is constructed by the coil technique, building the vessel by coiling long rolls of clay into the desired shape. The potter's wheel has never been used by the Indians. The pottery is then scraped and smoothed with a piece of dried gourd. Often a slip, a mixture of fine clay and water, is wiped on the surface to give a smooth surface. Final polishing is done with a smooth pebble before firing.

Designs, usually black or red and made of vegetable or mineral pigments, are painted on the unfired vessel with brushes made from yucca leaves.

Pottery is fired by placing it on a grate over a bed of coals. Cakes of dried sheep manure are then laid over the pile of pottery and allowed to burn. Firing lasts about two hours. Temperatures averaging about 1300 degrees Fahrenheit are reached in this primitive kiln.

Pottery fired in this manner tends to be porous. This is an advantage if it is intended for water storage. The evaporation of moisture seeping through the vessel keeps the water cool. However, before one can use Indian pottery as a flower vase, it should be waterproofed with paraffin or a plastic spray or provided with a glass jar as a liner.

The brightly-colored ware from Tesuque and Jemez pueblos is decorated with commercial poster paints. Much of this is not true pottery as the clay is not fired but merely sun dried.

NOTES & COMMENTS, continued.

CHIMAYO. Chimayo is a Spanish-American village in northern New Mexico. The name is applied to weaving done in this area by the descendants of the early Spanish settlers. These Rio Grande weavers use a foot operated loom with a flying shuttle. Chimayo weaving, which now makes use of machine-spun yarn, is not of Indian origin but is related to early Spanish traditions.

CHIEF'S PATTERN. Refers to the distinctive rug design shown above. Originally it was the pattern used in blankets worn by Navajo men. Whites often referred to them as "chief's blankets" although they were never used to denote rank.

KETOH (ga-toh). The Navajo name for the silver-mounted leather wrist ornament worn by the men of the Navajo and Pueblo tribes. Originally it was a simple device of fabric or leather worn by archers to protect the wrist from the snap of the bowstring. Its functional value ended with the introduction of firearms but it remained in use as an item of personal adornment.

PENDLETON. The trade name of a commercial blanket made in Oregon. Blankets and shawls from the Pendleton mills are great favorites among the Navajo and Pueblo Indians and are used to the almost complete exclusion of native weaving.

SUGGESTED READING

WORMINGTON, H. M. AND NEAL ARMINTA. *The Story of Pueblo Pottery*, Denver Museum of Natural History. Museum Pictorial No. 2, 1951.

MARRIOTT, ALICE. *Maria, the Potter of San Ildefonso*, U. of Okla. Press, Norman, 1940.

UNDERHILL, RUTH. *Pueblo Crafts*, U. S. Dept. of the Interior, Haskell Institute, Lawrence, Kansas. 1944.

OLD PAWN. Old pawn is a term used by collectors to denote fine early pieces of the silversmiths' craft. Most of these pieces were obtained as "dead" or unredeemed pawn from trading posts, hence the name. The term is often used today to refer to any item that has been pawned regardless of age. Contrary to popular myth, pawn jewelry is not a guarantee of superior quality. Old pawn is sought by collectors because of its historic interest, but junk as well as fine jewelry is pawned.

STERLING. Sterling is an alloy composed of 925 parts silver and 75 parts copper, an internationally accepted standard originally set by the British government. Coin silver generally runs between 900 and 915 parts silver. Indian jewelry is seldom stamped with the word "sterling." The silversmith sees no more reason to mark his product in this manner than he would label his moccasins "leather" or his pottery "clay." Indian silverwork is never plated.

GERMAN SILVER. German silver or sterline is an alloy of copper, zinc and nickel. It was introduced to the Indians by Europeans in 1850 as a cheap substitute for sterling silver. It is still popular among tribes in Oklahoma but is not used by Indian silversmiths in the southwest.

HIESHE (he-she). Hieshe is the word used by the Indians of Santo Domingo pueblo for necklaces made of shell beads.

WAMPUM. Wampum is a word from the Algonquin Indians of the eastern United States and refers to a tubular shell bead made from the center spiral of a conch shell. These beads were originally used in treaty belts and as ornaments. In the early 1600's the Dutch and English used wampum as a medium of exchange when there was a shortage of metal coins in the colonies. The term is now indiscriminately and incorrectly applied to all shell and turquoise beads in the Southwest. Beads are not "money" any more than an automobile, which also has a cash value, can be regarded as money.

JOKLA (zha-kla). The double loops of turquoise beads seen suspended from shell and turquoise necklaces are called joklas by the Navajo. Originally these were tied through the ear as earrings and hung on the necklace when not in use for that purpose. They are seldom used as earrings today but continue to be worn as part of the necklace.

CARE OF INDIAN CRAFTS, continued.

Do NOT put a Navajo rug into a washing machine. Rugs may be dry cleaned but be certain that the cleaner you send it to is experienced in the handling of Navajo weaving.

Rugs hung on the wall should be vacuumed occasionally and moth-proofed at least once a year.

If a rug is to be stored for any length of time, clean it first, then mothproof it and roll, rather than fold it, to prevent creasing.

INDIAN BASKETS can be washed by using detergent suds and a vegetable brush. Avoid soaking the basket in water as this dries out the fibers and makes them brittle. Old baskets which have become stiff and dry can be restored to life with several coats of mineral oil applied with a soft brush. Do not varnish or shellac Indian baskets.

SILVER JEWELRY should not be cleaned with paste polishes or "dips" as this removes all of the dark area in the design which is necessary to the appearance of the piece. A jeweler's rouge cloth will usually restore the luster to tarnished silver. Badly tarnished pieces can be cleaned with household ammonia and a toothbrush. Be sure to rinse well in clear water after scrubbing.

If the oxidized or blackened portion of the design is accidentally removed it can be restored by dissolving a small piece of "liver of sulfur" (available at most drugstores) in water and applying the solution to those areas with a small brush. Allow to dry before polishing the surface.

NAVAJO WEAVING, continued.
SUGGESTED READING

AMSDEN, CHARLES. *Navajo Weaving*, University of New Mexico Press, Albuquerque, Second edition. 1949.

BRYAN, NONABAH G. WITH STELLA YOUNG. *Navajo Native Dyes*, No. 2, Education Division, U. S. Office of Indian Affairs, Chilocco Agricultural School, Chilocco, Oklahoma. 1940.

DUTTON, BERTHA. *Navajo Weaving Today*. Museum of New Mexico Press, Santa Fe. 1961.

KENT, KATE PECK. *Navajo Weaving*, Heard Museum, Phoenix, Arizona. 1961.

MAXWELL, GILBERT. *Navajo Rugs, Past, Present and Future*, Desert Southwest Publishing, Palm Desert, California. 1693.

MERA, HARRY P. *Navajo Textile Arts*, Laboratory of Anthropology, Santa Fe. 1948.

MERRY, E. S. "So You Want To Buy a Navajo Rug?", *Indian Life*. Vol. 38, No. 1 pp. 30-35, Gallup, New Mexico. 1960.

Bead Making

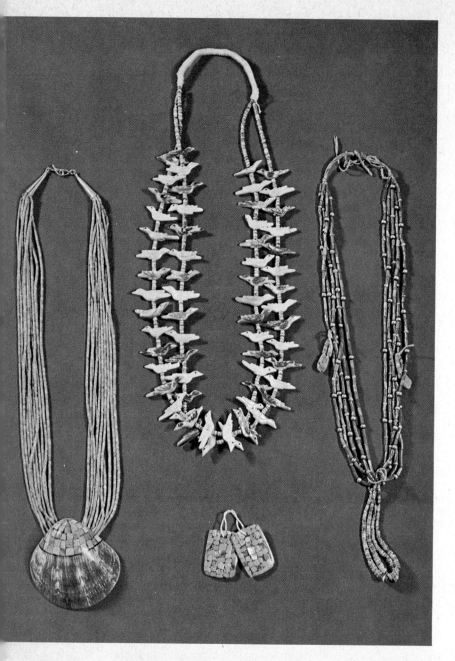

Bead making is an ancient craft that has been little affected by modern technology. The tools and techniques used today are essentially the same as those used long ago.

Sea shell, the most common material used for beads, has been an important trade item in the Southwest for over a thousand years. Clams, conus, abalone, olivella and spiny oysters are among the many species used. Most of these originate on the west coast of the United States and the Gulf of Lower California. These shells were carried inland over well-established routes by early Indian traders. Even in historic times tribes living in southern Arizona trekked across the desert to the ocean in search of shells and salt.

Beads are made by first breaking the shell into small irregular pieces. Each piece is then pierced with a hand pump drill. Thick shell is drilled halfway through from each side. The drilled fragments are strung on a cord and carefully rolled on a slab of fine-grained sandstone until they become disk shapes of the desired diameter. Turquoise beads are made by the same process. The smallest beads are the most expensive because they involve the most work. The color of shell beads ranges from white to silver gray and tan to dark brown.

The pueblos of Santo Domingo and Zuni produce all of the shell beads used in the Southwest today.

Coral beads, highly prized by the Indians, are cut and drilled in Italy. They were first introduced into the Southwest by the Spaniards as a trade item and continue to be imported for that purpose.

SUGGESTED READING

JEANCON, JEAN A. "Pueblo Beads and Inlay," Denver Art Museum, *Leaflet No. 30.* 1951.
Editor's Note—The Denver Art Museum's Indian Leaflet Series is an excellent source of information on all phases of Indian crafts.

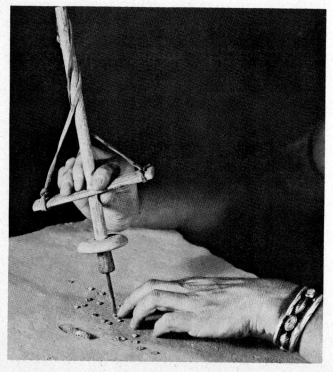

TOP. *Whole shells, decorated with a mosaic of turquoise or jet are often worn as pendants on shell necklaces. Bird fetishes are carved by the Zuni from shell and strung into necklaces. This form is of relatively recent origin. The rectangular pendants are a turquoise mosaic set into cottonwood. These were formerly worn as earrings by unmarried pueblo girls.* BOTTOM. *Drilling shell beads with a pump drill. Pressing down on the horizontal crosspiece unwinds the thongs and causes the center shaft to rotate.*